Dynamic

Dehydrator Recipes

An Illustrated Cookbook of Dehydrator Dish Ideas!

BY - Julia Chiles

Copyright 2019 - Julia Chiles

OOOOOOOOOOOOOOOOOOOOOOOOOOOOOOOOOOOOOOO

License Notes

No part of this Book can be reproduced in any form or by any means including print, electronic, scanning or photocopying unless prior permission is granted by the author.

All ideas, suggestions and guidelines mentioned here are written for informative purposes. While the author has taken every possible step to ensure accuracy, all readers are advised to follow information at their own risk. The author cannot be held responsible for personal and/or commercial damages in case of misinterpreting and misunderstanding any part of this Book

OOOOOOOOOOOOOOOOOOOOOOOOOOOOOOOOOOOOOO

Table of Contents

You can make some VERY delicious treats with your dehydrator, to take with you on the go. Try one of these great recipes soon…. 78

Introduction

Are you fairly sure you want to try a dehydrator, but not sure about forking over the money?

Consider these benefits of using a dehydrator:

- You can save money dehydrating your own foods. Buy vegetables, for example, when they are plentiful and less expensive, and use those dehydrated foods until the next harvest season.

- You can extend the shelf life of foods. Making your own fresh fruits will give you fruits that last for up to a year.
- Dehydrators are reliable and easy to use. They're really simple to use, and they rarely break down for years after their purchase.
- Dehydrators are pretty much foolproof. Since the temperatures you use will be low, it's difficult to leave food in for too long and over-dehydrate it.
- You can make healthy foods. Purchase locally grown bulk food and preserve it. You'll still be feeding your family real, healthy food.
- You'll be prepared for emergencies. No, I'm not talking about zombies. It's just good to have food stored for power outages and "rainy days". Turn the page and read on...

Rehydrating Dehydrated Foods and Meals

Recipes for dehydrating foods and meals do not generally include the instructions to rehydrate them when you're ready to use them. This section will provide you with simple steps that can basically be used whenever you rehydrate foods.

1. Choose the agent you'll use for rehydrating. It may be just water, or broth or juice. It depends on what you're rehydrating.

2. Fill your chosen rehydrating container with the liquid you'll be using to rehydrate your food. A bit too much water won't hurt your dried foods.

3. Check the temperature of your rehydrating fluid. You won't want it too hot. Some foods react poorly to hot water. Soak the dried food, leaving it for whatever time it needs to rehydrate fully.

4. Check on the rehydrating foods frequently. Don't remove it from water if it has an odd taste or a leathery feel.

5. Sometimes you can rehydrate as you cook a dried dish, like when you make soup. The meat and vegetables can be added as it cooks. The foods will rehydrate as your soup is cooking.

Here are some great breakfast recipes for foods you can dehydrate at home and fix while you're camping or otherwise away from conventional cooking sources...

1 – Camping Egg Breakfast

This recipe is fairly easy, as long as you make sure you don't use too much fluid to rehydrate the eggs. Once you've done it a time or two, it'll be easier – and they are delicious.

Makes 5 Servings

Cooking + Prep Time: 20 minutes + 8-10 dehydrator hours & 1/2 to 1 hour freezer time

Ingredients:

- 5 eggs, large

Instructions:

1. Crack the eggs in a bowl. You may need to split the amount for the size of your dehydrator trays.

2. Whisk eggs well, till blended fully and a bit foamy.

3. Carefully pour eggs into fruit leather dehydrator tray.

4. Dehydrate the eggs at 140F for 8 – 10 hours till flaky and fully dried. The egg flakes will be oily, so it should be easy to scrape them away without them sticking to tray when they have fully dried. If your eggs still feel sticky, leave sticky eggs in dehydrator for a short additional time period.

5. Transfer the dried egg flakes to zipper top plastic bag. Place in the freezer for 1/2 to 1 full hour.

6. Remove the eggs from the freezer. Blend in your food processor till fully powdered. They should not stick to food processor sides at all. If they do, they need to dry more. Put eggs in dehydrator again if they need more drying.

7. Store the eggs in a zipper lock plastic bag in a freezer till ready for use.

2 – Crunchy Breakfast Granola

When you buy boxed cereal, you're buying a processed food that contains little nutritional value. This granola is a REAL healthy breakfast.

Makes 16 Servings

Cooking + Prep Time: 35 minutes + 8 hours cooking time + 32 total hours dehydrator time

Ingredients:

- Water, purified
- 1 cup of pitted, packed dates
- 1/2 tsp. of salt, sea
- 2 & 1/2 cups of buckwheat groats, raw – soak for 8-12 hours, then rinse & drain, then sprout
- 3/4 cup of currants, raisins, cranberries, dried blueberries of cherries, organic
- 1/4 cup of seeds, flax – soak for 8-12 hours in a half cup of the water – don't rinse or drain
- 1/4 cup of pumpkin seeds, raw – soak for four to six hours, then rinse & drain
- 1/4 cup of sunflower seeds, raw – soak for four to six hours, then rinse & drain
- 1/4 cup of sesame seeds, raw – soak for four to six hours, then rinse & drain
- 1/2 – 1 cup of whole or sliced almonds, raw – soak for eight to 12 hours
- 1/2 – 1 cup of pecan or walnut pieces – soak for 8-12 hours
- 1 cored & wedge-cut apple, large
- 1 tbsp. of cinnamon, ground

Instructions:

1. Cover buckwheat groats in large bowl with one inch purified water. Allow them to sit for eight to 12 hours.

2. After the groats soak for eight for 12 hours, put groats in strainer or sieve. Rinse well. Allow them to sit in strainer in sink for eight hours more, so they can sprout. Rinse them halfway through the sprouting process. Rinse again before you add to recipe.

3. After groats are rinsed and strained, but before they have been left to sprout, put flax seeds and 1/2 cup water in bowl. Soak for eight to 12 hours. Seeds will mix with water, becoming a gel.

4. Place almonds, pecans or walnuts and salt together in separate bowl. Cover with water and soak for eight to 12 hours. Rinse, then strain. They will be done sprouting at the same time buckwheat has sprouted.

5. About half-way into soaking time for nuts and flax seeds, combine sesame, pumpkin and sunflower seeds in bowl. Cover with water. Allow to soak for four to six hours. Rinse, then strain. They will be done at about the same time as nuts and flax seeds are done soaking and buckwheat has completed its sprouting.

6. After groats, seeds and nuts are done, separate dates loosely. Soak in water for several minutes and soften if they seem too dry and hard. Drain off water. Remove pits.

7. Place dates and wedge-cut apples in your food processor. Add 1/2 cup water. Pure into paste with smooth texture. Add additional water if you need it.

8. Combine flax seed gel, dried berries or currants, raisins, groats and other nuts and seeds in large sized bowl. Add cinnamon, date paste and apple puree. Mix well, creating a batter.

9. Spread three cups of batter evenly, 1/4" thick or less, on dehydrator tray that is lined using wax paper or a sheet of silicone. Repeat till you have used all the batter.

10. Dehydrate the batter at 105 to 115F for eight hours. Flip the granola on clean hydrator tray. Remove silicone sheet or wax paper. Dehydrate at 105F for 24 more hours, till dry fully.

11. Break granola in chunks. Store in sealed jar in refrigerator for three months maximum. You can also keep the granola in sealed jars or storage bags in your pantry for a maximum for one month. Store till ready to use.

3 – Chocolate & Almonds Breakfast Smoothie

This smoothie is quite filling, and lactose-free. It's a great way to start your day. If you want a longer energy boost, you can add whey protein mix.

Makes 1 Serving

Cooking + Prep Time: 1/2 hour + 6-12 hours dehydrator time

Ingredients:

- 2 tbsp. of rolled oats or wheat berries
- 1 banana, whole
- 1 tbsp. of peanut butter or almond butter
- 1 tsp. of flax seed, ground
- 1 tsp. of powdered cocoa
- 3/4 cup of milk, almond

Instructions:

1. Combine all ingredients in food processor.

2. Process on high speed setting till frothy and smooth.

3. Spread on a dehydrator tray covered with parchment paper or non-stick sheet.

4. Dehydrate at 115 degrees F for six to 12 hours, till fully brittle and dry.

5. Remove from the dehydrator. Allow to cool.

6. Grind the dried smoothie mixture into fine powder in coffee grinder.

7. Pack recipe in small sized zipper top plastic bag. Store till ready to use.

4 – Pumpkin Lovers' Pancakes

I've never had a family member or friend who didn't like spicy, sweet pumpkin pancakes. They are especially tasty when you top them with honey or syrup.

Makes 1 Serving

Cooking + Prep Time: 10 minutes

Ingredients:

- 3 & 1/2 ounces of batter mix, pancake
- 2 tbsp. of pumpkin powder
- To fry: ghee (clarified butter)

Instructions:

1. Combine the mixture of pancake batter with pumpkin powder in zipper top plastic bag.

2. Pack the ghee separately. Store till ready to use.

5 – Sausage Breakfast Scramble

This sausage scramble has a bit of a kick to it, to help wake you up. It is a satisfying, hearty way to begin your day.

Makes 2 Servings

Cooking + Prep Time: 10 minutes

Ingredients:

- 4 tbsp. of pork sausage crumbs, freeze dried
- 4 tbsp. of crystal egg, whole
- 6 tomatoes, sun-dried
- 1 tbsp. of powdered tomato sauce
- 1/2 tsp. of oregano, dried
- 2 tbsp. of Parmesan cheese, grated, freeze-dried
- 1 tbsp. of ghee (clarified butter)

Instructions:

1. Mix the sausage crumbs, powdered eggs, oregano, powdered tomato sauce and sun-dried tomatoes in medium zipper top plastic bag.

2. Pack remainder of the ingredients separately. Store till ready to use.

There are all kinds of dishes you can dehydrate at home and prepare later. Here are some tasty main dishes, entrees, side dishes and appetizers...

6 – Pumpkin Wraps

Raw wraps are a tasty way to use dehydrated foods for quick meals. These wraps will be ready to eat in very little time, which is great when you're camping.

Makes 6 Servings

Cooking + Prep Time: 25 minutes + 5 hours dehydrator time

Ingredients:

- 1 chopped onion, red
- 2 cups of chopped pumpkin
- 1 cup of flax meal, fresh ground
- 1 cup of nut meal, almond
- 2 cups of water, filtered
- 2 tbsp. of yeast, nutritional
- 1/2 tsp. of powdered cumin
- 2 tsp. of garlic powder

Instructions:

1. This recipe Makes sufficient batter to fill 2 full dehydrator trays. You can make it in two batches if your food processor won't hold all the ingredients.

2. Blend water and pumpkin. Add remainder of ingredients, creating the batter.

3. Spread the batter evenly on a teflex sheet for dehydrator use.

4. Dehydrate batter for two hours at 145F. Remove it from dehydrator and place a second sheet of teflex and tray on top. Flip the batter over carefully. Peel first teflex sheet from dehydrator tray and dry underside of wrap.

5. Turn temperature of dehydrator down to 115F. Continue dehydrating for three hours.

6. Once wraps have dried fully and are still pliable, remove them from dehydrator trays. Slice wrappers into three rectangular strips. Store them in airtight container. This will keep them at least as pliable as they were when you removed them from the dehydrator. Store till ready to use.

7 – Barley – Beef Stew

This stew uses nutty barley, tender beef and a lovely array of healthy vegetables to make a truly great meal. The broth is so rich, it **Makes** this a popular stew.

Makes 1 Serving

Cooking + Prep Time: 10 minutes

Ingredients:

- 1/4 cup of ground beef, dehydrated
- 1/3 cup of cooked barley, dehydrated
- 1 tbsp. of carrots, dehydrated
- 1 tbsp. of green beans, dehydrated
- 1 tsp. of celery, dehydrated
- 1 tbsp. of powdered tomato sauce
- 1 tsp. of thyme, dried
- 1 tsp. of bouillon powder, low sodium

Instructions:

1. Mix all ingredients in med. zipper top bag.

2. Store till ready to use.

8 – Bulgur Dehydrated Chili

This vegetarian chili is delicious, hearty and healthy. Even meat lovers will enjoy it. Bulgur wheat is naturally low in fat and high in fiber, so it **Makes** the base for a healthy meal.

Makes 1 Serving

Cooking + Prep Time: 40 minutes + eight to 10 hours dehydrator time

Ingredients:

- 1/2 chopped onion, red
- 1 tsp. of oil, olive
- 1/2 chopped bell pepper, red
- 1/2 cup of diced tomatoes, canned
- 1/4 cup of bulgur, quick-cooking
- 1 tsp. of seasoning blend, Mexican
- Salt, sea
- Pepper, ground
- 1/4 cup of canned, drained kidney beans
- 1/3 ounce of chocolate, dark

Instructions:

1. Heat oil in pan on med. heat.

2. Add the onions. Cook till soft.

3. Add and stir in bulgur, peppers and the Mexican seasoning blend.

4. Cook for one to two minutes, releasing aroma.

5. Pour in one-half cup of water and the diced tomatoes. Bring to boil and stir occasionally. Season as desired.

6. Add kidney beans. Simmer for six to seven minutes, till nearly all the water has been absorbed.

7. Remove from heat. Cool down to room temperature.

8. Spread chili mixture on dehydrator tray lined with parchment paper or non-stick sheet.

9. Dehydrate for 8 to 10 hours at 125F till brittle.

10. Pack the dried meal in zipper top plastic bag. Store till ready to use.

9 – Kale & Carrot Cake Chips

Everyone seems to love these tasty, pleasingly sweet kale & carrot cake chips. They are a nice variation on typical cheese and salty flavored chips.

Makes 8 Cups

Cooking + Prep Time: 35 minutes + 8-12 hours dehydrator time

Ingredients:

- 3 cups of dried coconut, shredded finely
- 1 tsp. of salt, sea
- 3 tbsp. of agave nectar
- 1-2 tbsp. of syrup, maple
- 1 chunk-cut carrot, large
- 1 tbsp. of cinnamon, ground
- 1 tsp. of cardamom
- 1" chunk of ginger, fresh
- 2 tsp. of vanilla extract, pure
- Water, filtered
- 1/2 cup of dried coconut, shredded finely
- 1/2 cup of carrot, shredded finely
- 1 large, washed, torn bunch of kale

Instructions:

1. Combine coconut, salt, agave nectar, carrot, syrup, ginger, cinnamon, cardamom and vanilla. Process till you have a smooth mixture. Add a bit of water, as needed, till the mixture is thinner than typical nut butter.

2. Place kale in large sized bowl. Pour coconut mixture on top. Add shredded carrots and shredded coconut. Use your hands to massage this mixture into kale and make sure all pieces are entirely coated.

3. Place coated kale on two dehydrator sheets lined with teflex liners. Dehydrate for eight to 12 hours. Pour into zipper top plastic bags. Store till ready to use.

10 – Salmon & Cheese Pasta

If you like salmon, this is a great way to change up the way it's prepared. It's very satisfying, with a tangy, rich flavor, yet it's still easy to make.

Makes 1 Serving

Cooking + Prep Time: 10 minutes

Ingredients:

- 1 tbsp. of milk powder, full cream
- 2 tbsp. of powdered cheddar cheese, freeze-dried
- 1 tsp. of flour, all-purpose
- 2/3 cup of pre-cooked pasta, dehydrated
- Salt, as desired
- 1 tbsp. of ghee (clarified butter)
- 1 x 2 & 1/2 ounce pouch of salmon, smoked

Instructions:

1. Mix the flour, milk powder and cheese in small zipper top plastic bag.

2. Pack remainder of ingredients separately. Store till ready to use.

11 - Tomato Sandwiches

These sandwiches are SO popular around the campfire! They use cashew mayo to bring extra taste to juicy tomatoes, crisp lettuce and fresh onions.

Makes various # of servings

Cooking + Prep Time: 25 minutes + 3 hours of hydrator time

Ingredients:

For the Onion Bread

- 1 cup of water, filtered
- 1 cup of flaxseeds, ground
- 3 sliced onions, medium
- 2 grated carrots, large
- 1 tsp. of salt, kosher
- 3 tbsp. of oil, olive

For the Cashew Mayo

- 1 tsp. of agave
- 1/2 tsp. of garlic powder
- 1/2 cup of cashews

Instructions:

1. To prepare the onion bread, mix water with flax seeds. Allow to sit for a few minutes, till they have gelled.

2. Thinly slice onions. Grate carrots.

3. Stir ingredients together. Add salt.

4. Spread on pre-lined dehydrator sheets. Dehydrate for an hour or so. When the top feels a bit dry, flip over. Continue and dry other side. Allow both sides to dry for two more hours. It should be dry but not brittle. Cut bread. Place in zipper top plastic bags.

5. To prepare the cashew mayo, use blender to puree all the ingredients till creamy and smooth. Store all till ready to use.

12 – Italian Frittata

This simple Italian frittata recipe with sausage is a classic dish of cheese and tomato revamped into a dehydrator meal. You can easily make it ahead with your dehydrator and rehydrate it whenever you like.

Makes 1 Frittata

Cooking + Prep Time: 10 minutes

Ingredients:

- 6 tbsp. of whole eggs, powdered
- 1 tbsp. of milk powder, full cream
- 2 tbsp. of chopped tomatoes, sun-dried
- 1/4 tsp. of oregano, dried
- 1/4 tsp. of marjoram, dried
- Salt, sea
- Pepper, ground
- 1 tbsp. of oil, olive
- 1 shallot
- 3/4 ounce of chorizo
- 1 tbsp. of Parmesan cheese, grated, freeze-dried

Instructions:

1. Mix the dried herbs, tomatoes, milk and powdered eggs in zipper top plastic bag.

2. Pack remaining ingredients separately. Store till ready to use.

13 – Falafel & Garlic-Lemon Aioli

This is a delicious recipe that includes falafel balls along with a garlic and lemon aioli. The texture comes mainly from the carrots, flax and sunflower seeds. The spices combine with garlic and onion to give you bright taste in each bite.

Makes Various # of Servings

Cooking + Prep Time: 50 minutes + 2-12 hours dehydrator time

Ingredients:

For falafel

- 1 cup of sunflower seeds, dry
- 2 cups of carrots, chopped
- 1 cup of chopped parsley, fresh
- 1/4 cup of ground flaxseeds
- 3 tbsp. of onion, diced
- 1 clove of garlic, minced
- 1/4 tsp. of salt, kosher
- 1/2 tsp. of cumin, ground
- 1/2 tsp. of curry, ground
- 1/2 cup of sesame seeds – DO NOT add till remainder is processed

For garlic-lemon aioli

- 1/4 cup of cashews, dry
- 2 garlic cloves
- 1/8 tsp. of salt, kosher
- 1 fresh lemon, juice only

Instructions:

1. For falafel, add carrots only to your food processor. Process till carrots are almost the texture of a paste, chopped very well.

2. Add in garlic, flax seeds, sunflower seeds and spices. Process till mixed well.

3. Add parsley and onion. Be sure to scrape sides down and mix all ingredients together well.

4. Move mixture to large sized bowl. Add sesame seeds by hand.

5. Roll mixture into 1 tbsp. sized falafel balls. Place on dehydrator sheets. Dehydrate for two to 12 hours. If you want a moister falafel, leave in less time.

6. For the garlic-lemon aioli, process salt, cashews and garlic in spice mill till you do not have any chunks remaining.

7. Remove mixture from spice mill. Add to a bowl. Add lemon juice. Whip using a fork. Store till ready to serve.

14 – Chili Mac

Chili Mac is a delicious and nostalgic meal that warms you up and **Makes** you feel comforted. It's especially enjoyable in cold weather.

Makes 1 Serving

Cooking + Prep Time: 10 minutes

Ingredients:

- 1/4 cup of ground beef, dehydrated
- 2/3 cup of pasta, dehydrated, pre-cooked
- 1/4 cup of canned beans, dehydrated
- 2 tbsp. of powdered tomato sauce
- 1 pinch of chili powder
- 1 handful of Parmesan or cheddar cheese, grated

Instructions:

1. Mix the ground beef, pasta, chili, dried beans and powdered tomato sauce in medium zipper top plastic bag.

2. Pack the cheese separately.

3. Store till ready to use.

15 – Vegan Curry Wraps

These wraps make a wonderful lunch or snack, and they're quick to rehydrate. We especially love the fillings in this recipe, but you can substitute other favorites of yours, if you like.

Makes various # servings

Cooking + Prep Time: 10 minutes + 6-10 hours dehydrating time

Ingredients:

- 2 cups of water, filtered
- 2 cups of packed carrot pulp
- 1 & 1/4 tsp. of curry powder
- 1 cup of flax meal
- 1 tsp. of honey, organic
- 1 tsp. of coconut aminos
- 1/4 tsp. of salt, kosher
- 1/4 tsp. of garlic powder
- 1/8 tsp. of powdered cayenne

Instructions:

1. Add all the ingredients to food processor. Process till you have a smooth texture.

2. Evenly pour batter onto lined dehydrator trays. Form eight to nine-inch rounds, each about 1/4" in thickness. Leave 1/2 inch or more between wraps and edges of tray. Be sure batter is evenly spread.

3. Dry at a temperature of 115F for about four to six hours till wrap tops appear dry.

4. Flip wraps onto lined dehydrator tray.

5. Dry for two to four more hours and check on wraps every 1/2-hour. They should be flexible, but dry. Wrap edges will be cracked and harder. You can trim those edges off before you use the wraps, if you like. Store till ready to use.

16 – Taco Turkey Stew

There are LOTS of recipes available for taco soup, but this one is different than most. The turkey **Makes** it different and dehydrating means it's easy to make and serve.

Makes 4 Servings

Cooking + Prep Time: 1 & 1/4 hours + 8-12 hours dehydrator time

Ingredients:

- 2 & 1/4 pounds of turkey mince, lean
- 1 tbsp. of oil, olive
- 2 chopped bell peppers, red
- 1 chopped onion, red
- 1 x 14-oz. can of drained black beans
- 1 x 12-oz. can of drained sweet corn
- 1 packet of spice mixture, taco
- 1 x 14-oz. can of tomatoes, diced
- Salt, kosher, as desired
- 1 bunch of chopped cilantros, fresh
- 1 tbsp. of powdered cheddar cheese, freeze dried
- 1 handful of crumbled corn chips

Instructions:

1. Heat oil in large sized pan. Add onions. Cook till golden and softened.

2. Add turkey. Cook till it has fully browned. Transfer to colander. Drain turkey. Return to pan.

3. Add corn, beans, red pepper and taco spice blend.

4. Stir occasionally as you continue cooking for five minutes or so.

5. Add diced tomatoes and juice. Bring to boil.

6. Add cilantro. Season as desired.

7. Reduce the heat down to low. Place lid on pan. Allow to cook for 15 more minutes.

8. Remove from heat. Allow to thoroughly cool.

9. Spread turkey stew on pre-lined dehydrator trays.

10. Dehydrate at 145 degrees F for eight to 12 hours, till stew is brittle. Allow it to cool.

11. Divide dried meal in equal portions in separate zipper top plastic bags. Store till you are ready to use them.

17 – Vegetable Pulp Pizza

This recipe is an awesome way to use up leftover pulp. It helps you get more from your produce and juice.

Makes 8 pieces

Cooking + Prep Time: 10 minutes + 15 hours dehydration time

Ingredients:

- 16 ounces of vegetable pulp
- 1 & 1/4 cup of flax meal
- 1 cup of water, filtered
- 2 tbsp. of tamari
- 1/4 tsp. of salt, sea
- 3 cloves of garlic
- 1 jalapeno pepper
- 1 bell pepper, yellow
- 1/2 cup of yeast, nutritional
- 1 fresh lemon, juice only

Instructions:

1. Blend together all the ingredients with the exception of sesame seeds.

2. After mixture is well mixed and creamy, sprinkle the seeds around the crust.

3. Spread on a dehydrator sheet. Dehydrate at 115F for 15 hours or longer. Store till you are ready to use.

18 – Irish Stew

Traditional Irish stew is one of the backbones of typical Irish cuisine. It's hearty, filling, and most of all, delicious!

Makes 1 Serving

Cooking + Prep Time: 10 minutes

Ingredients:

- 1/4 cup of potatoes, dehydrated
- 1/4 cup of canned beef, dehydrated
- 2 tsp. of carrots, dehydrated
- 1 tbsp. of green beans, dehydrated
- 1 tbsp. of fried onions, dehydrated
- 1 tbsp. of powdered beef gravy
- 1 tsp. of thyme, dried
- 1 tsp. of bouillon powder, low-sodium

Instructions:

1. Mix all ingredients in medium zipper top plastic bag.

2. Store till ready to use.

19 – Kelp Noodle Bok Choy Pad Thai

This dish sounds like it might be difficult to make, but it's not. You'll season it lightly using lemon and coriander, and the marinated Bok Choy **Makes** the ensemble a complete and delicious meal.

Makes various # of Servings

Cooking + Prep Time: 40 minutes + 1-2 hours dehydrator time

Ingredients:

For the Bok Choy

- 1 tbsp. of oil, olive
- 1 bunch thinly sliced baby bock choy
- 1 pkg. of separated mushrooms
- Salt, sea & pepper, ground, as desired

For the Pad Thai

- 1/3 cup of oil, coconut
- 2 tbsp. of almond butter, raw
- 1 tbsp. of liquid aminos
- 1/2 de-seeded jalapeno pepper
- 1 tsp. of coriander, ground
- 2 tsp. of lemon juice, fresh-squeezed
- 1/3 cup of water, purified
- 1 pkg. of noodles, kelp

Instructions:

1. Sprinkle Bok Choy with mushrooms and olive oil. Toss and coat well. Season as desired.

2. Spread mixture on dehydrator tray lined with teflex. Dehydrate at 95F for 1 to 2 hours.

3. To prepare Pad Thai, combine all ingredients except kelp noodles in food processor. Process to a sauce-like, smooth texture.

4. Drain, then wash kelp noodles. Cut into shorter pieces, as desired. Combine noodles with Bok Choy and mushrooms in large sized bowl. Pour sauce over top. Mix well. Store till you are ready to use.

20 – Mushroom Stroganoff

This is another classic comfort food that's even easier to make with a dehydrator. It pairs well with mashed potatoes, pasta or rice.

Makes 1 Serving

Cooking + Prep Time: 10 minutes

Ingredients:

- 1 tbsp. of milk powder, full cream
- 1 tsp. of flour, all-purpose
- 1/2 tsp. of thyme
- 1 tbsp. of ghee (clarified butter)
- 2 tbsp. of mushrooms, dried
- 1 shallot, small
- Salt, kosher
- Pepper, ground

Instructions:

1. Mix the flour, powdered milk, mushrooms and thyme in medium zipper top plastic bag.

2. Pack the remainder of the ingredients separately. Store till ready to use.

21 – Spicy Green Beans

These green beans can be used in recipes, but they also make a very tasty snack all by themselves. Make some up for long car rides – your family will thank you!

Makes various # of servings

Cooking + Prep Time: 25 minutes + 1-2 hours dehydrator time

Ingredients:

- 1 pound of beans, green
- 1 tbsp. of oil, olive
- 1/2 tsp. of salt mix, spicy

Instructions:

1. Bring pan of water to boil.

2. Add the green beans. Blanch for three to four minutes.

3. Remove beans from stove. Plunge green beans into cold, filtered water so the cooking process stops.

4. Dry off beans. Toss with oil and the spicy salt.

5. Place the beans on drying trays in a single layer. Set dehydrator to 125F. Dehydrate for 1-2 hours. Store till ready to use.

22 – Easy Seafood Curry

If you like seafood, this dish will be a favorite. It starts out with a tasty, healthy curry sauce that goes so well with the fish.

Makes 1 Serving

Cooking + Prep Time: 10 minutes

Ingredients:

- 1/4 cup of basmati rice, cooked, dehydrated
- 1/4 cup of seafood mix, dehydrated
- 1 tsp. of curry paste, Thai yellow, dehydrated
- 2 tbsp. of powdered tomato sauce
- 3 tbsp. of powdered coconut milk

Instructions:

1. Mix all ingredients in zipper top storage bag. Store till ready to serve.

23 – Chili Con Carne

This dish can be served in so many ways! It can be spread on bread or crackers, or for guests, a baked French baguette.

Makes various # of Servings

Cooking + Prep Time: 25 minutes + 8 hours dehydrator time

Ingredients:

- 2 or 3 chili peppers, hot
- 1 tomato, ripe
- 1/2 cup of parsley, fresh
- 1/4 cup of dehydrated seeds, mixed
- A bit of oil, olive

Instructions:

1. Mix seeds with tamari. Place in dehydrator tray at 115F for 8 hours.

2. Peel tomato. Remove liquid and seeds. Cut flesh into small pieces.

3. Cut parsley in small pieces, too.

4. Spread oil on your fingers. Slice chili peppers.

5. Mix all ingredients. Store in the refrigerator in glass jar till you're ready to serve.

24 – Raw Camping Veggie Burgers

These raw veggie burgers are satisfying and savory, and amazing when served with favorite fixings in lettuce wraps. It's a filling meal and made with only vegetables, herbs, nuts & spices.

Makes 18 Burgers

Cooking + Prep Time: 25 minutes + 5 to 6 hours dehydrator time

Ingredients:

- 1 & 1/2 cups of pecans
- 1 & 1/2 cups of almonds
- 4 carrots, large
- 1 brown onion, medium
- 2 handfuls of parsley, fresh
- 3/8 cup of lemon juice, freshly squeezed
- 1 & 1/2 tsp. of salt, kosher
- 1 & 1/2 tsp. of tarragon
- 3 tsp. of rosemary, dried
- 2 tsp. of curry powder, mild

Instructions:

1. Chop onions and carrots roughly.

2. Add all ingredients to your food processor. Process till well mixed and finely chopped.

3. Use your hands to shape mixture into burgers.

4. Dehydrate burgers for 5 to 6 hours at 140F. Turn burgers one time after 2 hours. Store till ready to use.

25 – Raw Mushroom Casserole

This dish starts with two types of mushrooms and adds onions and sun-dried tomatoes. It's topped with a tasty walnut crumble that **Makes** it unique.

Makes Various # of Servings

Cooking + Prep Time: 50 minutes + 2 hours dehydrator time

Ingredients:

For the vegetables

- 10 sliced mushrooms, cremini
- 2 sliced Portobello mushrooms
- 6 tomatoes, dried – soak for 1 hour, then drain and slice
- 1/2 diced onion, small
- 1 tbsp. of tamari
- 1 tbsp. of oil, olive

For the sauce

- 2 tbsp. of yeast, nutritional
- 8 mushrooms, Cremini
- 1 or 2 minced cloves of garlic
- 1/4 cup of water, filtered, +/- as needed
- 1/4 cup of pine nuts
- Salt, sea, as desired
- 1 tbsp. of rosemary, fresh
- 1 tbsp. of thyme, fresh

For the crumble topping

- 1/2 cup of soaked, dried walnuts
- 2 tbsp. of yeast, nutritional
- 1 minced clove of garlic
- Salt, sea, as desired

Instructions:

1. Combine mushrooms, 1/2 onion and tomatoes in large sized bowl. Toss with oil and tamari. Place on lined dehydrator sheet.

2. Dehydrate for one hour, till soft.

3. Add second 1/2 of onion to food processor, plus 2 tbsp. yeast, water, garlic, Cremini mushrooms, pine nuts, herbs and sea salt. Process till you have a smooth texture and set mixture aside.

4. Combine the garlic, yeast, walnuts & salt in food processor. Process till chopped finely. Add a bit of water till mixture begins clumping together.

5. After vegetables are soft, combine in bowl with sauce. Pour into shallow dish. Top with crumble. Dehydrate for another hour. Store till you are ready to serve.

You can make some VERY delicious treats with your dehydrator, to take with you on the go. Try one of these great recipes soon...

26 – Fake Butterfinger Bites

These treats are not made with Butterfinger® bars, but you sure would think they are when you taste one. They are SO addictive, too.

Makes 3 dozen balls

Cooking + Prep Time: 25 minutes + 4-5 hours dehydrator time

Ingredients:

- 2 cups of peeled, then cored & chopped apples, dried
- 2 cups of coconut
- 2/3 cup of peanut butter
- 1 & 1/2 tbsp. of vanilla, pure
- 1/4 cup of powdered cocoa

Instructions:

1. Add ingredients to large sized bowl. Combine thoroughly. Shape into 1/2-inch to 1-inch balls. Roll them in the cocoa powder.

2. Dry in dehydrator for 4 to 5 hours at 135F till crisp on outside and firm. Store till you want to use.

27 – Raw Lime Coconut Macaroons

You'll want to sink your teeth into these lime & coconut macaroons, dipped in chocolate. The outside is crunchy, and the inside is chewy – they taste amazing.

Makes 12 Servings

Cooking + Prep Time: 55 minutes + 12 hours hydrating time

Ingredients:

For the macaroons

- 3/4 cup of almond meal, raw
- 2 tbsp. of lime zest, organic
- 2 tbsp. of lime juice, fresh
- 1 pinch salt, sea
- 1/4 cup of agave nectar, raw
- Several leaves of spinach
- 2 cups of unsweetened coconut, shredded finely

For the chocolate

- 1/4 cup of cacao powder, raw
- 1/4 cup of coconut oil, raw
- 2 tbsp. of agave nectar, raw
- 1 pinch salt, sea

Instructions:

1. To prepare macaroons, place the almond meal, lime juice, lime zest & salt in food processor. Process till combined well.

2. Add spinach and agave nectar. Process till mixture is holding together. Add coconut. Pulse till mixture holds together well.

3. Form mixture in 12 balls. Place on dehydrator sheet and dehydrate for 11-12 hours, till dried. They should still be chewy in center.

4. To prepare the chocolate, whisk all the ingredients together till smooth. Allow to set till it has thickened a bit. Lay out sheet of aluminum foil on sheet pan.

5. Dip macaroons into chocolate. Place on foil. Once you have dipped them all, place in freezer so they can set. They can be eaten once chocolate hardens. Store in refrigerator till use.

28 – Apricot & Almond Butter Cookies

I wasn't sure these cookies would be as good as the version that includes chocolate chips. They are JUST as good and in some ways better, since the almond butter and apricot flavors have a chance to shine.

Quantity varies by size of cookies

Cooking + Prep Time: 35 minutes + 8-12 hours dehydrator time

Ingredients:

- 1 cup of butter, almond
- 1 cup of apricots, dried
- 1 cup of unsweetened coconut, shredded
- 1 handful of dates, Medjool

Instructions:

1. Add apricots and dates to food processor. Pulse and chop. Add almond butter. Blend till texture is fairly smooth.

2. Add coconut. Pulse till dough can be rolled into balls. Add a bit more coconut or water, as needed.

3. Roll out into small sized balls, about a quarter's size in diameter. Use all dough.

4. Flatten dough balls in hands to make cookies 1/4-inch thick. Place the cookies on 1 piece of parchment paper.

5. Place paper and cookies on trays in dehydrator. Run at 155F for 8 to 12 hours. Store till ready to use.

29 – Raw Brownie Bites

These brownie bites get their sweetness from dates, so they're healthier than brownies made with refined sugars. They are vegan and paleo friendly, too.

Makes various # of bites

Cooking + Prep Time: 30 minutes + 15 hours total dehydrating time

Ingredients:

- 3/4 cup of flour, almond
- 3/4 cup of flour, coconut
- 1 & 1/2 cup of milk, almond
- 1/2 cup of powdered cocoa
- 1/2 cup of dates, Medjool

Instructions:

1. Mix the cocoa powder, coconut flour, dates and almond meal in food processor.

2. Add almond milk and process.

3. Scoop onto dehydrator tray lined with drying sheet.

4. Dry at 145F for three hours. Lower temp. to 110F. Allow to dry for six hours.

5. Remove drying sheets. Continue to dry for six more hours. Store till ready to use.

30 – Fig & Date Balls

These fig & date balls make a wonderful snack to grab and take with you when you're on the go. I usually have some rehydrated on Monday to use as healthy weekday snacks.

Makes about 30 balls

Cooking + Prep Time: 30 minutes + 4-6 hours dehydrator time

Ingredients:

- 1 cup of dates, dried
- 1/2 cup of figs, dried
- 1/2 cup of raisins
- 1/2 cup of prunes
- 1 cup of walnuts, crushed
- 1/2 cup of sunflower seeds
- 1 cup of coconut
- 3 tbsp. of lemon juice, fresh

Instructions:

1. Grind the raisins, prunes, figs and dates finely in food processor.

2. Mix ground fruit with nuts and seeds in medium sized bowl. Add and stir lemon juice.

3. Shape dough in 1/2-inch to 1-inch balls. Roll them in the coconut. Dehydrate at 135F for four to six hours or till outside is crisp. Store till ready to use.

Conclusion

This dehydrator cookbook has shown you...

How to use different ingredients to affect unique ready-made tastes in dehydrated dishes both well-known and rare.

How can you include dehydrated dishes in your home recipes?

You can...

- Make campground eggs and pancakes, which I imagine everyone knows about. They are just as tasty as they are at home.
- Learn to cook with pre-dehydrated foods, which are widely used in dehydrator recipes. Find them at big box stores, local markets and online.
- Enjoy making dehydrated dishes that include many types of meat. Meat is a mainstay in this type of cooking, and there are SO many ways to make it great.
- Make delicious, dehydrated soups and stews, which are often made in dehydrators.

- Make various types of desserts like lime coconut macaroons and raw brownie bites, which will tempt your family's sweet tooth.

Have fun experimenting! Enjoy the results!

Author's Afterthoughts

Thanks ever so much to each of my cherished readers for investing the time to read this book!

I know you could have picked from many other books, but you chose this one. So, a big thanks for reading all the way to the end. If you enjoyed this book or received value from it, I'd like to ask you for a favor. Please take a few minutes to ***post an honest and heartfelt review on*** *Amazon.com.* Your support does make a difference and helps to benefit other people.

Thanks!

Julia Chiles

About the Author

Julia Chiles

(1951-present)

Julia received her culinary degree from Le Counte' School of Culinary Delights in Paris, France. She enjoyed cooking more than any of her former positions. She lived in Montgomery, Alabama most of her life. She married Roger

Chiles and moved with him to Paris as he pursued his career in journalism. During the time she was there, she joined several cooking groups to learn the French cuisine, which inspired her to attend school and become a great chef.

Julia has achieved many awards in the field of food preparation. She has taught at several different culinary schools. She is in high demand on the talk show circulation, sharing her knowledge and recipes. Julia's favorite pastime is learning new ways to cook old dishes.

Julia is now writing cookbooks to add to her long list of achievements. The present one consists of favorite recipes as well as a few culinary delights from other cultures. She expands everyone's expectations on how to achieve wonderful dishes and not spend a lot of money. Julia firmly believes a wonderful dish can be prepare out of common household staples.

If anyone is interested in collecting Julia's cookbooks, check out your local bookstores and online. They are a big seller whatever venue you choose to purchase from.

Made in the USA
Coppell, TX
17 December 2023

26395085R00059